Keys To Success For Kids

Caleb Maddix

Keys To Success For Kids
By: Caleb Maddix

Copyright © 2015 by Matt Maddix Motivations

WARNING – DISCLAIMER

Edited by Pam Eddings

Cover design by Dee Cole

Table of Contents

Endorsements

Caleb Maddix is the most dedicated and hardest working young man that I've ever had the pleasure of coaching and knowing. Whether in sports or daily life, he strives to be the best at it by outworking everyone else. Keep up the good work, kid.

Steve Schwarz
Caleb's Hitting Coach

While most young men his age are focused on video games and snap-chatting, Caleb Maddix has an uncommon focus on success. I've had the privilege to work with him on several humanitarian and social justice projects, and I have great respect for his passion to reach outside of himself to help others. His unique perspectives coupled with a powerful work ethic have enabled him to accomplish great things early in life. Caleb's poise and acumen are inspiring, and people of all ages will benefit from his insight.

Mike Hopkins
Family Friend

I have had the distinct honor of knowing Caleb Maddix for several years now. It's truly a pleasure to see a young man filled full of **energy** and **passion** at his age. I have owned and managed multiple companies for over 10 years, and I cannot wait to see what the future holds for a youth who has found the same vigor that I have used for many years. I fully endorse this book and Caleb Maddix. Best wishes my friend, and always remember, "People who are crazy enough to believe that they can change the world, are the ones who do!

Respectfully,
Robby Tarver

Caleb is without a doubt a one-of-a-kind young man. Caleb is not your average 13-year-old. He speaks with confidence and has a sense of focus and purpose. There are some people in this world who have the ability to set a goal and achieve anything in life they want to. Caleb is one of those people. No matter your age or expertise in life, I trust you will be motivated and inspired by Caleb's attitude to find the Keys to Success.

Josh Combs
Children's Pastor, Evangelist
Manchester, CT

Among Caleb Maddix's many virtues and good qualities, the one that impresses me the most, is his sincere love for the things of God and passion for God's Kingdom! Caleb is a well-mannered, thoughtful, hard-working young man, with a heart for helping people. He is a disciplined 13-year-old with a dream, who has applied himself to helping other kids. His heartbeat to help others has expanded into his own organization called "*Kids With a Mission*!" While many teenagers are confused and easily influenced by the wrong things, Caleb's hunger after God has kept him on the right pathway! He loves to study and read the Bible, and for several years now has given short "messages" that have inspired his listeners to do positive things for God! He has focused his energy to fulfill a dream: to write a book and share the "wisdom" he has gleaned in his few short years, so that other kids can be helped, enlightened and inspired to reach for their dreams! **"Keys to Success for Kids"** will be a great read for all children and young people. I applaud Caleb for this wonderful accomplishment!

Joy Haney
Author, Speaker

Growing up I was held to a higher standard than other kids my age. Whether I was on the field or off the field, I was taught to carry myself with confidence, always give everything I have to what I am doing, and treat others the way I would want to be treated. For the past few months, I have had the pleasure of working with Caleb, whose standards are the same. It's awesome to see such a young dude have such a good head on his shoulders. Big props to his parents for raising him well. As far as baseball skill and talent, Caleb is a great athlete with good actions and a solid mind for the game. The attribute that will take him further in his baseball career is his work ethic. I've never seen a kid other than myself work so hard and consistently as Caleb. That kind of person is destined to be successful at whatever he does with his life, baseball or not. I'm very happy our paths crossed and can't wait to continue to get after it in the offseason with him.

Dante Bichette Jr.
Caleb's Baseball Trainer, and Baseball Player for the New York Yankees

I have known Caleb literally his entire life. I have watched him grow up into the amazing young man that he is today. I truly am amazed at his natural ability to be positive, motivated and goal driven. I have never met anybody who can be as focused to achieve what they want as Caleb. He is driven to grow every day and learn about how to be successful. He constantly reads and cares for other people. On a vacation, he came up with the idea to help the homeless in New York City. Caleb Maddix is special, unique and gifted. I recommend this book to everyone that can read, not just kids.

Travis Worthington
Family, Mentor

Chapter 1

Excuses Be Gone

During a recent afternoon in school, I had some free time to read an assigned book, but as often happens, my mind drifted away from the book into another world... I was thinking... well, who knows what I was thinking? Then suddenly, my attention came back to the classroom and I began to hear one person saying, "I can't" while another said, "I don't want to." The final sentence I heard was, "It is too hard." I realized the students were complaining, but I didn't allow the complaints to linger in my mind. I was so used to hearing these words that I didn't let it affect me.

A couple hours later in Physical Education (P.E.) class, the memory of those words in the earlier class was revived when my gym teacher assigned laps to everyone based on their behavior during the beginning of class. He went through the names, and my friends all had 1 lap.

When I finally heard my name called, my coach said, "Caleb Maddix, three laps."

Out of shock I screamed, "WHAT!!!!" I was in disbelief that all my friends had only one lap when they were acting exactly the same as I was. Can you believe that? That was so unfair!!!!

"That is all the names, go run your laps," said my coach.

As I ran my laps, I found myself mumbling under my breath words just as bad as the ones I had heard earlier in the day in the other class. This time I heard myself say,

"This isn't fair," and "They talked just as much as I did," and other words on the same scale as those.

All of a sudden, I remembered something I had heard when I was watching some keys to success lessons on YouTube. The video said, "No one determines the quality of your life but you."

I realized that this applied here. I deserved the 3 laps, and even though I thought my friends deserved 3 as well, their assignments had nothing to do with my attitude. Even if my friends did run 3 laps, I would still have to run the same amount of laps, in the same amount of time, at the same place. My attitude automatically changed. I realized I was making excuses. Yes, my friends deserved laps, and yes, their smaller assignments might have been "unfair," but I really did deserve the laps I got. I decided to change my attitude. That decision brings us to our first key to success.

Key to Success: When something doesn't go your way, blame yourself first.

I've noticed that many kids tend to make excuses, but very few of them admit that they do. It is important for you to recognize and acknowledge the excuses you make each day. To find out what excuses you use, try the drill below.

EXCUSE LIMITING DRILL: Go to school and keep a record of how many excuses you make throughout the day. Do this for a week, and then try to lower the amount of excuses you speak each day. It would be helpful to set a goal of the total number of excuses that you would allow yourself to make. What helped me overcome excuse-making was setting rewards and consequences based on the number of excuses that I would make. The ultimate goal is to get to the place where we don't make any excuses and take full responsibility for our actions. It's important to hold yourself to a high standard and become the type of kid that refuses to make excuses.

I realize things are going to happen; it may not always be your fault, but no matter how bad a situation is, you can always change your response to it.

Key to Success: Things will happen to you, but you always have control of the situation.

This doesn't mean that if something unfair happens to you, you have magic fairy dust to make it fair. But you can always change something, and that something is your ATTITUDE toward it. There is never a good excuse for failure to succeed or failure to be happy. There is always a way. Someone once said, "Life is 10% what happens to you and 90% how you respond to it." When something happens that doesn't go our way, find a way to maintain a positive and enthusiastic attitude.

Your words are powerful in situations. In the same manner that you can bully people with actions, you can also bully someone with words. Now you may not think you're a bully, but believe it or not, you can bully yourself by saying words like, "I can't," "I won't," "It's impossible," "I am bad at it," etc. These words are powerful and are hurtful to you. Get rid of these excuses as soon as possible. Once you remove those junk words from your life, you can surely succeed.

This may seem hard, but the following word is the key to your success in this area.

RECOGNIZE: If you do the drill I mentioned earlier in this chapter, you will have already recognized what your excuses are, but knowing what they are is not enough. You must also recognize and admit that you are wrong. This is probably the hardest part in the process because no one wants to admit they are wrong. However, this step is a must if you are going to get rid of the excuses you speak on a regular basis. Recognizing also has to do with the fact that when you do hear yourself saying an excuse in your head or out loud, you take a deep breath and go through this check list.

✓ Am I in this situation because I did something wrong?

✓ Am I blaming something besides myself?

✓ How can I change the situation now?

✓ What can I learn from it?

Key to Success: When you recognize that you made an excuse, go through the excuse checklist.

Let's give it a try with this example:

You are in Science class and your teacher tells the class not to talk during the assignment. One minute later, your friend asks you for help on problem #4. You help him, and your teacher hears you explaining how to do the problem. She reminds you that you were instructed not to talk, and she assigns consequences for disobedience. You get mad and say, "That is not fair. I was helping him." Suddenly, you realize you just made an excuse for your behavior. Your first reaction this time should be to apologize to your teacher as soon as you recognize your attempt to excuse your behavior. Then go through your checklist and answer the questions.

✓   Am I in this situation because I did something wrong?

○   Yes, she told me not to talk, and I disobeyed and talked anyway.

✓   Am I blaming something besides myself?

○   Yes, I am blaming my teacher for getting me in trouble for not doing anything. I am also blaming my friend because he asked me for help and made me talk when in reality I made the choice to talk and get in trouble.

✓   How can I change the situation now?

○   I can go to the teacher after class and apologize for displaying a bad attitude.

✓   What can I learn from it?

○   From now on when my teacher tells me not to talk, I won't talk.

Following this checklist will teach you to recognize and eventually eliminate your excuses in your journey to the successful life you desire! Always be willing to grow and learn. The final reminder for this chapter is this:

When you hear excuses come out of your mouth, tell them…

"EXCUSES, BE GONE!!!"

Chapter 2

Goal Setting

Big Problem:

We have learned how to stop making excuses and take control of our life, but there is no reason to have control of our life if we don't have something to succeed at. I go to different places all around the country and see kids. I ask almost every kid that I meet this question. "What do you want to succeed at in life?" Almost 90% of the time the answer is, "I don't know." In my opinion, that is the worst response to ever give to that question. I couldn't imagine my life without a goal. It would be like floating in space with no purpose, no dream, and no destiny. If you don't know what your goal in life is, what your purpose is, or what you are going to master/succeed at, then you are going to find out in this chapter.

With the help of my parents, I created a business organization called "Kids with a Mission" (which I will discuss later in this book). One of our business goals is for every kid to have a "mission" on this earth. You are never too young to know what you are going to master and have a plan in place for how you are going to master it. In fact, everyone in this world should know what their goal is.

"Caleb, why?" You may ask when reading this.

Because if you go through life without a dream, or something to accomplish, one day you are going to be at a gas station telling people the price for the peanuts they are buying. And you are going to ask yourself, "Do I enjoy waking up in the morning? Am I happy? Have I made an impact on anyone?" The answer to every one of those questions will be a resounding, "NO"!!!! That will be the answer to anyone who has a job other than their dream job. That doesn't mean you need to be scared; it should motivate you because you have an edge. You can start to work at your craft now. As a kid, try to find your passion when you are as young as possible. For example, I am only thirteen, but I knew what my goal and passion was by the time I was seven. Knowing what your goal is will help keep you focused even at a young age. Then when you get out of college (if you go to college, that is), you won't end up wondering where to go or the next step to take. Now it is okay if you don't know what your next step is right now. It is certainly okay if you don't know what your goal is. Most people don't. However, if you are one of those kids who don't know what your goals are, let me give you some tips for discovering your passion and calling.

How to figure out what your long term goal is:

Before you determine what your goal is, you need to understand that you may not have the same goal as your parents, friends, teachers, or anyone else. You are going to have your own personal goal. You will have your own dream. Don't let anyone tell you what your dream is going to be. Take advice from people, but a long term goal has to be something you are passionate about. It is important that you believe in your dreams and that you are confident of them regardless of those who try to talk you out of them.

While speaking to college students, Jim Carrey made a great statement. He said, "I have learned that you can fail at doing something you don't love, so you might as well do something you do love."

The journey to success should be fun! Make your goal something you love and could do every day of your life. You should be happy when you have to "work" to reach your goal because you know what you are going to accomplish. Your motivation should be your love for the goal and the process of achieving your goal. When you wake up in the morning, you should not feel discouraged. It should be the opposite. When you accomplish one of your goals, you should feel excited! There will be times where you feel lost and think there is no chance you can accomplish your goal. That is what we call the **GRIND.** To be honest, the grind is a good sign that you are on the right path to success. Everyone experiences the grind, but the person who keeps grinding will succeed. When determining what your long term goal is, don't forget that the ultimate goal is to please God and be of service to others. God does say that without a vision, the people perish in Proverbs 29:18. When thinking of your vision, dream, or goal, ask yourself these questions.

Where am I now?

To answer this question you must be honest with yourself. If you don't understand the question, I will ask it in an easier way to understand. What abilities do I have? What am I good at? And the most important, what do I love doing? Once you answer these questions, think of how you could potentially make that your career or a goal to accomplish.

What do I want to do?

Don't choose a goal only because your parents or teachers or someone you respect is telling you what to do with your life. Listen to their advice and wisdom, but also choose something you enjoy and will gladly commit to pursuing. Also, you must make sure that you have a reason why you want to accomplish your goal. For me I have decided to make sure that all my goals and dreams are in alignment with the Bible. For example, say your goal is to open a coffee shop. Every Saturday you could give out free coffee to the homeless. Whatever it is, make sure you give God the glory through it. God will bless that. Your career goal should also be something practical that will produce income for you. Dream big! Don't have a small goal; make it something that is almost impossible to accomplish. If you set your goal for the moon and fail, you at least will make it to the sky; but if you set your goal for the sky and fail, you will only be a couple feet off the ground. Dream big and don't let anyone tell you that you can't accomplish it! You will do it if you believe and start getting your jet pack ready to soar to your dream.

How will I get there?

Accomplishing your goal will require focus and hard work. You will need to do something every day to accomplish it. You will need to develop a routine which we will talk about in the next chapter. You will need to get rid of things and make sacrifices. You will need to be committed. I cannot fully tell you how to accomplish your goal or how to get there in this chapter. As you read through this book, you will be given specific ideas to help you understand how to ACCOMPLISH your goal. I look forward to being able to teach you some keys to success. One of the keys to success for this second chapter is commitment. The real way to accomplish your goal is to be COMMITTED and love what you do to the point where you WILL MASTER your craft. The secret to mastering your craft is consistent practice and hard work.

How will I know if I have accomplished it?

It is very important that you know when you accomplished your goal. Is it when you make a million dollars? Is it when you get a new car? Is it as small as getting straight A's? Your goal can't be something like wanting to be the greatest singer ever. It has to be something that is specific. It could be something like wanting to win the most music awards. Then when you win the most music awards, you will know you have accomplished your goal.

Key to success - You need to set a date for accomplishing your goal. I have learned that I get more results when my goals are specific and I have a clearly defined deadline. For example, if you want to run a mile in seven minutes, you should set a goal that is specific with a deadline that says, "I will run a mile in seven minutes by Sunday, December 13, 2015 at 5 pm."

How many goals can I have?

You can have as many goals as you want as long as you stay focused on your main goal. Perhaps you want to attend a certain college. It is okay to also have a goal of getting an A in Math or a goal like doing thirty-five push-ups. In fact, I recommend having other smaller goals. I actually think it is impossible to succeed without smaller goals. You need to have little goals along the way. If your goal is to play in the NBA, then you can have goals liking making your high school team or making your college team or starting on your college team. Whatever the large goal is, you should have smaller goals along the way.

What's holding me back?

I talked earlier about getting rid of things and making sacrifices to succeed. This might be the single hardest thing to do on the path to success. Why? Because over the years people create bonds and get attached to things and people they shouldn't. Everybody does, but if you are going to succeed, you must get rid of those things. It may be hard, but it is worth it to be honest and ask yourself what is hindering you from success. You must get rid of it, or none of this book matters.

What advantages do I have to get to my goal?

Now this is very important because you need to get an edge on your competition. What strengths do you have? How can you be better than your competition? You can always outwork them! Derek Jeter said that hard work beats talent if talent doesn't work hard. You must work hard, and you must grind! It is very important to know if you have an advantage. Advantages may be found in the people you know or the resources you have. You need to find your strength and advantage.

Who can help me?

As you journey on your road to success, you will need to have a mentor. You need to find a mentor if you don't have one. There are a lot of bumps and obstacles on your way to success, so you need someone to be there. I have about 8 mentors. Get as many as you can. Learn something from everybody. In searching for a mentor, look for someone who is successful in the areas you want to achieve. If you want to open a cupcake shop, but you don't know how to make cupcakes, you could go to your local cupcake store and ask the person who makes the cupcakes if they could give you a lesson every Monday on how to make a cupcake and how to run a cupcake store. You could pay them $20 a lesson, and they would be happy to teach you, but you need a mentor to help you reach your goal. It's very important to show your mentors that you are eager to learn. My dad has taught me that you should never be in the presence of your mentors without asking good questions. It's been helpful for me to write a list of 10-20 questions that I want to ask every one of my mentors. For example, here are some questions that I would ask one of my mentors.

1. What are the top three books that you would recommend for me to read?

2. What was the hardest lesson you had to learn on your path to success?

3. If you had to live your life over again, what would you do differently?

4. What's one area that I can improve in my life?

5. Why do you think most people fail to reach their goals?

You should try to learn something from everyone you meet. For example, some of the greatest lessons that I ever learned about baseball, I've learned by asking this question to the umpires and the coaches of the teams that we play against, "What is your best advice for a young baseball player?"

Key to Success: Have something to remind you of your goal every day. If you want to become a policeman, you could go online and print a picture of a policeman and put it on your door so that you are reminded everyday of your dream. Derek Jeter, a baseball player who has won the World Series five times, wanted to be the shortstop for the Yankees, so when he was a kid, he hung a Yankees uniform on his bedroom wall, and every time he walked in his bedroom, he was reminded of his goal. He accomplished his goal and played baseball for 20 seasons as the starting shortstop for the Yankees. It is important for you to have something to remind you of your goal so you work to accomplish it every day.

Key to success: If your parents allow you to use YouTube, find videos that give instructions for the goal or goals you are pursuing. I use it every day to study baseball tips. Whatever your goal is, look up instructional videos for that subject. YouTube can be a mentor. For example, some of the people I study are Mark Cuban, Michael Jordan, Derek Jeter, Jack Canfield, Tony Robbins, Dustin Pedroia, Dante Bichette, Jr. and others who are successful in their craft. Since I play baseball, I am going to study people who have been successful in baseball. If you are a hockey player, you might study someone completely different, but YouTube can be a big help.

Chapter 3

Developing a Routine

What is a routine? A routine is the backbone of your goal. It creates the flow for your day. It keeps you on track for what you want to accomplish. While some mistake a routine for a schedule, it is not. Many days are crazy, and it can seem impossible for the average American to have a set schedule of how their day will be. Many things change throughout the day. That is why I don't like to teach kids to have a schedule. Although a schedule might be helpful for some, I would much rather teach the practical principle of developing a ROUTINE.

Definition of routine: a sequence of actions regularly followed or something you do every day. I like to teach that your routine should be 5, 10, 15, or 20 things you do every day to accomplish your goal. My routine includes five things I do every day.

- Do my baseball drills and training.

- Juice fruits and vegetables.

- Pray, read my Bible, and meditate.

- Do my workout *routine.*

- Spend an hour on personal growth.

My routines are simple, but I do them every day: it ends up paying off in every area of life.

Note: I have routines for different things. I have an overall routine, and then I have a baseball routine. But part of my overall routine includes my baseball routine. You can have routines for different items to get things done.

How to set up a personal routine:

Start with your "Big Rocks"

The story is told of a time management professor who, while teaching on the importance of prioritizing, used a jar that would hold five gallons of liquid to illustrate his point. He had fist-size rocks on the desk, and he put them in one by one until he could not fit any more rocks. He asked his class if the jar was full and since he couldn't fit any more rocks inside the jar, the class answered a loud "Yes!!!!" Listening closely to the class he said, "Are you sure?" Then he pulled out a glass of gravel and poured it in. Next, he poured in a glass of sand and ended by pouring a glass of water over the gravel, rocks, and sand until it was full to the top. All the students were shocked! The point of the story is not how much you can fit into the jar. The point is that you had better put your big rocks or your important items in your day before you let the fillers of life fill the jar.

Routines ensure that you accomplish the important items in your day before small stuff gets in the way and distracts you. When developing a routine, simply think of the important things you must get done to be successful. Think of what will matter in ten years and then put that in your daily routine. Not video games or TV, but things that really matter. Don't worry about the small things; you will still find time for the little pebbles like video games or TV.

When developing your routine, you need to make it somewhat fun so you will want to do it every day. Sometimes though, you have to do things you don't want to do in order to help you reach your goal. My routines help me to be healthy, have a good relationship with God and people, become better at baseball, and develop strength. Yours need to help you in the areas in life that are most important.

Make it practical

You have to make sure your routine is something you can do on a daily basis. My parents are divorced, and my five routines vary each day depending on where I am. For my baseball workout at my dad's house, I hit baseballs he pitches to me, but at my mom's house, I do my hitting drills by hitting off the Tee into a net that my dad set up for me, and I do my wall drills. This may be the same for you. Say you are on a road trip and one of your goals might be to play football. You could just watch football drills in the car on the road trip. You have to find a practical routine that you can make happen every day. Sit down and write out a routine. Do not miss a day.

Note for success - REWARD YOURSELF! It is important that you find little ways to reward yourself at certain times for doing your routine so you will want to do your routine each day. If you do your routine every day for a month, allow yourself to watch an hour of TV or something else that you enjoy doing.

Backup Routine

I have a backup routine because I often travel with my dad when he speaks. I also have baseball events often, and sometimes it is hard to fit in all the "Big Rocks." Also, because I am constantly going back and forth between my dad's and my mom's houses, it can be difficult for me to do the same routine each day. So I have learned that it can be helpful to have backup routines to use when I am in different situations.

I. Scenario #1: At my dad's house

A. Do ab workout, jog, arm and leg workout

B. Hitting baseballs: Dad does soft toss, and I hit off the tee. Fielding part of baseball: Dad and I throw long toss (long toss is when we throw from a super far distance), and Dad rolls or hits ground balls to me.

C. Pray, read my Bible, and meditate.

D. Dad juices for me.

E. Get in an hour of personal growth.

II. Scenario #2: At my mom's house

A. Ab workout, jog, arm and leg workout

B. Hitting baseballs: I do my wall drills and hit off the tee. I throw a ball off the wall and use a pancake glove (flat baseball glove), then I throw the ball off the wall and use a normal glove.

C. Pray, read the Bible, and meditate.

D. Mom fixes fruits and veggies for me.

E. Do an hour of personal growth.

III.   Scenario #3: On the road for a trip, or if it is impossible to get outside to do my normal routine.

A. Pull over and do ab, arm and leg workout.

B. Watch YouTube baseball training videos and study different techniques of baseball. Take dry cuts inside if I can find space. Visualize myself fielding and hitting.

C. Pray and read the Bible.

D. Find a local juice bar or drink the juice that my dad has already pre-made for our road trip.

E. Call or text someone to connect.

Those are my scenarios, and I recommend you develop a routine for good and bad scenarios so that you never get caught being unable to do your routine. It might be hard to find time, but you <u>MUST</u> MAKE IT HAPPEN!!

<u>How routines can help you achieve your goal</u>

When I was eight years old and just starting to play baseball, I was not very good at it. All my friends were much better than me, and I did not get to play much. I was devastated! One day while complaining to my Dad, he told me something that still sticks with me today. This was the secret my Dad told me that all successful people know. My

Dad said, "Son, I know it may be hard for you not to play much, but it won't help to just sit and complain about it. The only reason that the other kids are better is because they practice a lot. They work harder than you. If you really want to be good and start on the team, you will have to work. I will be willing to help you, but you have to want to do it. I will not make you. If you really want to be good, you need to set a goal and find a good routine so you can accomplish your goal."

"What is a routine?" I asked curiously.

"A routine is something you do on a daily basis no matter what happens." My Dad said he was glad his son was so eager to learn. That was the day I learned an important secret to success. Hard work! That is a real secret to success.

My Dad taught me later that day that you can't just work hard without a purpose. So we set a goal. You might be curious and wonder what the goal was. It was that I would make the All Star team that next year. Not only did I make the All Star team, but I was also the starting shortstop for the All Star team. Now that may not seem like a lot, but for a kid who doesn't even start on his own team, at that point it was kind of dreaming big to say that he would start as shortstop for the team that has the best players in the league altogether. I wasn't worried about how big of a dream it was. My dad had always taught me to dream big. As I mentioned earlier, if you shoot for the moon and fail, you will make it to the sky; but if you shoot for the sky and fail, you will only make it a few feet off the ground. We also developed a routine and every day for the next year, my dad and I practiced our baseball routine. When the whole season was finally over, I felt like I played really well. Our coach of the team said he was going to call the three all-stars on our team at some time the next day. Of course, I waited anxiously for a call. By 3:00 pm I still hadn't received a call, and my heart was full of disappointment. When it was 8:00 pm, I knew I had to face the truth. I was going to say it, but my dad beat me to it. He said, "You worked really hard, and I thought you deserved to be an All Star, but I don't think you made the team. Maybe next ye———." He was cut off by the phone ringing. It was my coach. My dad looked at me kind of in shock and excited at the same time.

The phone rang the kind of ring that sort of said to my Dad, "Ha, got you! You thought I wouldn't call." My Dad picked up the phone. I was about to burst, but I didn't because my Dad was on the phone.

I heard a muffled voice on the other side of the phone. I wanted to hear what it was saying, but I couldn't make out the words. All I could hear was, "Don't worry———Ok–He will be glad to hear it." My Dad paused in between each sentence. He hung up the phone and said with a smile and a dance in the same sentence, "You made the team." I was so excited I let out a yell and did a little victory dance as well. I'm not the best dancer, so I probably looked kind of silly, but I didn't care. I was an All Star!!! Dad interrupted me with the caution, "Don't get too happy now; you haven't accomplished your goal yet young man. Your goal was to be the starting shortstop for the All Star team."

•••

"Are you ready?" asked my Dad.

"To be honest I am a little worried," I replied.

"Don't be; you will do great and have fun. Just remember all we have worked on. Fast bat, quick feet, and be respectful to the coaches."

"All right, how far are we? I want to be one of the first people to the All Star practice."

"Actually we are here. Let's go warm up so we can get some grounders in before practice," Dad said.

We took groundballs and hit a little before practice started. My new All Star coach was nice to me and introduced himself. We started off the practice by huddling up, and each team shared their names. After that, the coach had us go out to the positions we were assigned. I was glad when my coach had me and one other kid go to shortstop. Although the other kid was very good, I had confidence in myself. We took groundballs and played as the cutoff man on relays to second, third, and home. The other shortstop and I were about equal in our skills. Really there was no saying who was better. He would make a nice play. I would make a nice play. It was too close to tell who was going to start. Practice ended after we went to batting practice. I met my dad at our car, and we got in. "Our team is really good, I said."

"You guys are," my Dad replied.

"I didn't want to bring it up right away, but who do you think is going to start shortstop?" I asked.

"It is hard to tell. You guys are equal," he said. "Caleb, you have three weeks of practice left," Dad declared, then paused.

Impatiently I said, "What is your point?"

"If you really want to start shortstop, how are you going to do it?"

Impressed, I knew the answer to that question, so I said, "By having good form and charging the ball."

"Though that can help if you really want to start shortstop, you need to work ten times harder than him. Lately you have been slacking off on your routine," Dad said.

"You're right. I will outwork him and will start shortstop!" I said enthusiastically.

After three weeks of doing my routine every day, we had our first game. I was in the dugout when my Coach was yelling out the lineup. The only thing that stood out to me that I could really hear was "Caleb Maddix, batting second, playing shortstop!"

"Yes! I am playing shortstop!!!!" I screamed.

●●●

As you can see, it is very important to develop a routine, and it will lead you to the road to success. That is just one of many stories of how a routine has changed my life. I went from being a really average baseball player to the starting shortstop of the All Star team. I will never forget this valuable lesson. Achieving our goals doesn't come easy, but if you develop a routine and stick with it, you will be unstoppable!!!!

Chapter 4

Be Different

Being a kid in the world today can appear difficult. Why? Because we are taught to be the same as everyone else. We are constantly told that who we are is not cool. We get picked on in school when we do not wear the right shoes. Being different is almost forbidden. If we try to be ourselves someone is there to tell us that who we are is not good enough. This happens to the point where we forget what it means to be different or to stand out. That is why I am here. I am going to teach you the importance of being different and how it can be a huge key to your success. If you stick with me, you can finally stand out. I am going to give you "12 Keys to Being Different." Before I do, I must warn you. If you follow all twelve keys, two things will happen. It will bring people to you, and it will push people away. What that means is that when you decide to be different, some people may not like you because you are different, but others will like the fact you are different and will become your friend. If you truly want to succeed, you might have to let go of some friends; but once you succeed, you will have true friends that don't care how different you are from most people.

Let us get into the twelve steps to help you stand out so you can be on your way to success.

1. Decide what being different means for you.

It is very important to understand what standing out in the crowd means, but to be honest, it is not the same for everyone. For some, it may be their talent that stands out to people. For others, it may be their work ethic, ability to be a leader, manners, or maybe even their energy level. Everyone has something different that stands out. For me, it is my work ethic. Whatever your strength is, embrace it. The true way to stand out is to show your strength. Most people hide it; do not be that person. Let it go. You must find what makes you stand out. It may be multiple things or just one thing, but in order to succeed, you have to be different because the people who try to fit in don't succeed. Whatever stands out for you, run with it.

2. Think for yourself.

Being different will not happen if you think the same as other people. Sometimes you will come up with ideas that people find stupid. You will think differently, but do not hide it. Voice your ideas. Some people are what we call *small-minded thinkers*. These are the people who tell you that you can't, but do not listen to them. Smile at them and say, "You watch and see." Small-minded thinkers also are the ones who don't believe in dreaming big; instead they try to think *practically*. Someone who was a small-minded thinker was Dr. Lee De Forest. On February 25, 1967 he said, "Man will never reach the moon regardless of all future scientific advances." Two years later on July 20, 1969, Neil Armstrong and his crew took a step on the surface of the moon. This NASA crew proved Dr. Lee De Forest wrong. It wasn't just Dr. Lee De Forest who said they couldn't do it; it was the whole world, and the whole world is a pretty big crowd. They did not listen to the crowd; they thought for themselves. They had an idea, and they succeeded. If they can do it, you can do it. You may only have a couple of friends who think it is weird that you are different, but the astronauts had the whole world. Think for yourself. Don't think like the crowd.

3. Don't let the crowd hold you back.

The crowd will try to keep you back from success. They will try to get you to be like them. They will try to tempt you. They will try to get you hooked on the newest fad or gadget. If you want to succeed, sometimes you have to ask yourself, "Will this thing help me or hold me back?" Some people can look like they have it all but really hate their life. Don't give in to what they try to get you to do. It will hurt you if you let it. Be safe, and be smart. Don't let anyone or anything hold you back. Stand out. When successful people see you being different, they will respect you.

4. Take risks.

In order to be successful you must be willing to fail. Most people are afraid to fail. Life is not about how much you fail; it is about enduring through failures. I cannot name a successful person who has not failed. Just to give you a word picture, here is a long list of successful people who have failed.

Henry Ford, founder of Ford Motor Company, failed five times before achieving success.

R. H. Macy, founder of Macy's Department Store, had seven failed businesses before succeeding.

Soichiro Honda, founder of Honda Car Company, was turned down by Toyota and was jobless until he succeeded.

Bill Gates, CEO of Microsoft and the richest man in the world, dropped out of college and started failing in business until he created Microsoft as we know it.

Colonel Sanders, founder of KFC, had his chicken recipe rejected 1,009 times before it was accepted.

Walt Disney, founder of Disney, was fired from his newspaper job because he wasn't creative, and his ideas were considered bad.

Albert Einstein, perhaps the smartest man ever and Nobel Prize winner, didn't say his first word until he was four years oldand couldn't read until he was seven; that caused his parents and teachers to think he was handicapped, slow, and anti-social. He was also expelled from school.

Thomas Edison, inventor of the light bulb, was told he was too stupid to learn anything. It also took him 1,000 unsuccessful attempts before producing a successful light bulb.

Oprah Winfrey, richest woman ever and a TV icon, was told she was unfit for television.

Harrison Ford, starred in many movies including "Star Wars" and "Indiana Jones," was told by film executives he did not have what it took to be an actor.

Elvis Presley, famous musician and singer, was fired after one performance, and his manager said, "You ain't going nowhere, son. You ought to go back to driving a truck."

Michael Jordan, no doubt the greatest basketball player ever, was cut from his high school basketball team.

I could go on forever, but I think you see my point. You should never be afraid to fail. The greatest people in the world fail. Why? Because they take risks, and in order to get what successful people have, you must do what successful people do. Take risks.

"You miss one hundred percent of the shots you don't take." – Wayne Gretzky

5. Do things many people won't do.

The way to stand out is to do things most people won't do because if you do what they do, you look the same. If you are trying out for your baseball team and miss a groundball, you could ask the coach to hit you another one. You have to do what no one else does so you can get to where no one else is going. How do you do that? By being different. You are never going to get halfway to success if you do not shine. There are millions of kids that are the same as you. The way you get the edge is by standing out.

6. Have good manners.

Although you may think manners are unnecessary, they are very important. When people see you use good manners, they respect and remember you. It is different from what most kids do. Something my parents really stress is for me to use my manners. Here are some basic examples of how to use good manners.

- **Saying "Please"** when you want something. Not only will it be respectful, but people also become more generous in giving to you.

- **Say "Thank You"** when someone does something for you. It makes people feel appreciated.

- **Say "Excuse me"** when you bump into someone. Don't give them a dirty look like they did something wrong. Also, when you leave a table or need to interrupt a conversation, remember to excuse yourself.

- **Say "I'm sorry"** and be willing to admit when you are wrong. This is not easy to do, but we all make mistakes and should take responsibility for them.

- **Saying "Yes Sir" or "Yes Ma'am"** will go far with adults. Never answer an adult "yeah" or "no."

- **Give up your seat** if you are somewhere crowded and see an elderly or disabled person, an adult, or (for guys) a female who is standing. A true gentleman would say, "Please take my seat." My dad has always taught me that if they say no, I should stand up and say, "Please, I insist that you take my seat!" Even if they don't take the seat, I still feel that a gentleman should remain standing.

- **Don't chew with your mouth open because it is disgusting**.

- **When you eat, do not put your elbows on the table,** but before a meal and after meal, it is acceptable.

- **Use your phone when it is an appropriate time.** Also, when conversation is going on around you, engage in it instead of texting or playing games.

- **Open doors for everyone who is behind you.** If you open doors for people, who knows what doors they may end up opening for you? Waiting for others to go first is a quality that really stands out to other people.

7. Keep your word.

It is very important to keep your word. If you want to succeed, you must be honest and always tell the truth. People do not appreciate being lied to, so if you are trustworthy, they will respect you.

8. Take action when no one else does; be a leader.

Being a leader instead of a follower is important because if you follow the crowd, that could lead to destruction. What does it mean to be a leader?

- **Think like a leader.**

Leaders think confidently. Thinking confidently means you act like you belong. Don't sit there and think that the crowd is cooler than you are; believe in your God-given abilities, and no matter what people say, just smile and think, "I am going to be a leader, and I am going to be successful." Often the names of soldiers are forgotten, but the names of generals are remembered. Why does the general stand out from everyone? Because the general is the leader.

Leaders also think firmly. Leaders make up their mind and stick with it and don't let anyone tell them it is impossible. They are firm and stand their ground.

39

Leaders think progressively. In other words, they are constantly maturing and learning. They have the ability to answer, "I don't know" once, but rarely twice. When they are unsure, they think, they research, and they learn. Leaders are learners!

Leaders are positive. When a group around them is complaining and making excuses they say, "Guys we've got this," "Complaining won't help," or they solve the problem. Wherever they are, they turn a negative into a positive.

Leaders think compassionately. Leaders care about people and know how to be a servant. The Bible says, "He that is greatest among you shall be your servant" (Matthew 23:11). If you want to be great, you have to serve and be compassionate.

- **Act like a leader.**

Leaders are caring. They are interested in their followers and are willing to help them learn.

Leaders are committed. They are committed to succeeding. They will do anything and everything to reach their goals, and they will help other people reach their goals, as well.

Leaders are curious. They are constantly asking questions. My dad often tells me that you can learn something from everyone, so ask questions of everyone. Leaders grow and are curious to learn more.

Lastly, leaders lead by example. A smart leader knows it is important to show the way and not just tell everyone how to do it. Your example by actions means more than any words you will ever speak.

- **Put it all together.**

Leaders are constantly improving the world. They identify problems in the world, and try hard to find ways to solve them. They also share their vision with people. They will often have a fan base and many followers. You can be different and have a ton of people who will follow you. Being different is a good thing, and your true friends will stay with you.

9. Be confident in yourself, and always be humble.

In order to stand out you must be confident in your abilities. Don't compare yourself to anyone. You can only compare yourself to the person you were yesterday. Keep progressing, and be confident that you can handle pressure and succeed. I see so many people on social media saying, "I hate being ugly," "I am so fat," "I have no friends," etc. I can't stand it. It makes me so irritated. They have no confidence. Please do not be this person. Be confident, but not prideful. You are not better than anyone, and we all have room for improvement. Be yourself. Stand out and be who God made you to be!

10. Communication skills.

Your communication skills are very important. They are the first impression you have on people and sometimes the only impression. You will meet a lot of people in your life, and some of them may be very important. Some of the important people may have a big part in your success and may be able to impact you greatly. I assure you, if you take these tips to heart and follow them, people will be very impressed by how different you are from other kids and will respect you for it. They may even help you succeed. Also, you never know who you are talking to when you meet a stranger, so you better always respect each and every one of them. Let's start with tip #1 for improving communication skills.

Tip #1: Eye contact

This is the tip my dad stresses to me the most. He tries to get me to look everyone I meet in the eye. I struggle with this because I get so interested in my surroundings. My dad has always told me that looking someone in the eye does four things:

- Shows you care.

- Shows you respect them.

- Shows you are listening to them.

- Shows you have confidence.

Many kids nowadays don't care, respect, listen, or have confidence. When people see you do those things, they know something is different about you. They recognize you are going places, and they will be more willing to help you if you look them in the eye.

Tip #2: Introducing yourself to people

Introducing yourself is a very simple process. First, identify the person you are going to introduce yourself to and ask yourself questions like, "Are they in higher authority than me?" "Are they male or female?" These questions will come in handy later. Then, all you have to do is walk up to them with confidence, look them in the eye, and say, "Hello, I am (insert first and last name)." If you say your first and last name, people are more likely to remember you.

Tip #3: Names

After you have introduced yourself, ask them their name if you don't already know it. Now this is where the questions that you asked yourself when you first saw them come in handy. If they ended up giving you their first and last name and are an adult, then you call them Mr. or Mrs. _____. If they are younger than you, then call them by their first name. Out of respect to grown-ups, you will want to use a respectful title. Other than knowing when to use Mr./Mrs. or their first name, it is very important to remember the name of the person you are talking to. There are many techniques to remembering names. One of the ways to remember people's names is to imagine throughout the whole conversation that their name is written on their head. It will associate their name with them and when you see them, their name will kind of pop up in your memory.

Other ways to remember them is if you have a friend or relative that has the same name as they do, you can imagine you are talking to that friend or relative. If you ever see the person again and you remember their name, they will feel appreciated. One more thing about names is throughout a conversation with someone, it is very important that you use their name often. Make comments like, "(insert name), what do you think about this painting?" Use their name before questions often. You do not want to overdo it though. One last tip about names is to use their name before and after a conversation. For instance, "Hello, Lucy. How are you?" Or "See you later, Lucy. It was nice to talk to you."

Tip #4: Handshaking

Once you meet someone it is very important to give them a handshake. You should shake their hand right when you tell them your name. How firm your handshake is will vary depending on who it is. Here is a little scale.

- Elderly women = Not hard

- Elderly Man = medium

- Women = A little bit above medium

- Man = Firm, but not as hard as you can

Giving a handshake will tell people that you are mature and mean business. It shows that you are a well-mannered person.

Tip #5: Volume when speaking

It is very important to speak up and not sound timid, but this does not mean to scream. All it means is to speak loud enough for the person to hear you clearly, but not everyone in the whole building. Speak up, but not too loudly.

Tip #6: Body language

What is body language? Body language is communication from the movement or attitude of the body. Basically, what it means is that you tell people things by the way you act.

My dad told me that you can tell more from body language than from what is coming out of a person's mouth. That is true. You can tell if someone is sad or happy just by how they look. If I told you I was sad right now, what do you think I would look like? Probably slouched down, head down, moving my head back and forth. You can almost imagine what I look like just because you know I am sad. What if I told you I was sad, but I was smiling? You would probably say I am not sad. It is all about how we act and look. Anytime you are down, do not show it. Always smile, and eventually you will start to be happy. Really, try it sometime! People want to be around someone who smiles and is happy because they will end up feeling that way. Positive moods are contagious! If everyone is sad, try to smile and pick them up because with good body language, you can change people's days for the better. In addition, people will say, "Man, he is always happy." Next time you are down, change your body language and attitude, and you will change how you feel.

Make sure when you communicate to people that they see that you are mature and that you are different. Most importantly, they will see that you are happy. It will bring people across your path that will eventually help you.

11. Be a servant.

This is so important to me because of the mission God has given us to be servants. No matter how high you get to your goal, you always need to be willing to serve. If you truly want to succeed, you need to be able to serve others. Any time you get a chance to serve, take it. Our overall goal should be to serve as much as we can. We are all privileged and someone always has it worse. It is up to us to help that person who is perhaps less fortunate. We must have a servant's heart. Never forget to serve. God blesses those who serve, and people respect the one who serves even when it isn't expected. Serving is not just feeding the homeless. It may be picking up a water bottle on the ground or helping your friend with a situation in their life. You can always find a way to serve.

12. Be an encourager.

People usually need help to feel better about themselves, or maybe they have had a rough day. As leaders, we need to be there to encourage them. Sometimes you can make someone's day just by simply saying something nice. You never know who needs encouragement, so give it to everyone. People like hanging out with the person who encourages others. The people who encourage are the ones who are different. They are the ones who stand out. They are the ones who will succeed. One word of encouragement might make someone remember you for a lifetime. Go out of your way to be kind. You will not regret doing it, but you may regret not doing it. Anyone can be negative and tear people down, but successful people know the art of being an encourager.

Chapter 5

Personal Growth

I hope you take this chapter very seriously because this will have an enormous impact on your success. You always have to be willing to grow, but before you can, you must first know that only you can grow yourself. That is why we call it PERSONAL growth. It is you personally growing. Throughout this chapter, I will give many keys on how to grow, but you must take action and want to learn. You can learn something from anybody and anything, and you are never too successful to learn. No one knows everything, so you should always have a passion to learn.

A good definition of personal growth is doing *activities* that help achieve one's goal. These activities may include listening, reading, watching, studying, thinking, relaxing, etc. People strive to grow in many areas in life. Some focus on health while others may focus on money or relationships, but all of them have something in common. What is it? They all have determined what needs improvement in their life and have made up their mind to make those changes. This leads us to the first step of personal growth.

Decide what you want to change in your life. I know that most adults are the ones focusing on this, but it is good to develop the right habits while we are kids. I just graduated from being a kid and am now in the teen club. One thing I remember was that people treated us too much like *kids*. Because of the way we were treated, we ended up developing the idea that we don't have to worry about *real life* yet, when in reality the age we are at now is the most important. I want to get that idea in you. You are not *really a kid*. In some countries we are considered adults, and while we should do fun things and be a *kid,* we should be taught that in life we need to know more than what 5+5 is; we should also be taught about how to succeed, how to improve, and how to grow. I want you to know, I AM HERE TO HELP. I am going to teach you how to grow. You already know the first step. **Decide what you want to change in your life.** What do you want to improve? Right now don't worry about how you will do it. I will talk about that later. Focus on what you need to improve. What is it? It may be your grades. It may be your attitude. Whatever it is, think about it. STOP HERE until you have in mind what you want to improve in your life. By the way, there may be multiple things you want to improve; that is great. I think everyone who is honest with themselves will admit that they need to change many things about their life. We are going to go through a step-by-step process to improve the things that are holding you back from full success.

Step 1: We already went over step one, but just to make it clear, I will do it again. You need to figure out what changes need to occur for your personal growth. Some questions to help you answer that might be:

- What do I need to change in my life?

- What area do I feel is the weakest in my life?

- What areas in my life need to be improved?

- What things would I like to learn that I have never studied before?

Step 2: Choose the resources that will help you grow and create massive success in your life. This is achieved by simply asking, "What things will help me learn?" I have many tools that have helped me grow. I am going to share six of those tools with you.

1. Books

I speak for myself when I say books have greatly impacted me. I mean, why would I write a book if I thought books were worthless? You can learn so much from books. People fit so many tidbits for success in a book. If you read a book on success, I guarantee you will learn at least one thing that you can take into your life and apply. Many successful people share their secrets on how they achieved success in books. As a kid, I'm not sure why we don't use that to our advantage. We all are looking for the key to open the door to our success. We all want to know how people have opened the door to success. It shocks me that we don't realize people literally have drawn a key to the door and put it in a book, yet we never take out the key and use it. Could it be that we don't want to go through the whole process of reading the whole book?

"The more that you read, the more things you will know. The more that you learn, the more places you'll go." - Dr. Seuss

<u>3 Books Kids **Must** Read</u>

1. The Bible is by far the most important book you will ever read because it contains the greatest wisdom for success.

2. *Positive Dog* – Jon Gordon

3. *Success Principles for Teens* – Jack Canfield

How to Get Books to Read

Getting books today is so easy. You can do four things.

1. Buy a book from a bookstore.

2. Download books on your iPad or phone.

3. Amazon is a great place to order books online.

4. Visit your local library.

I recommend downloading books to your iPad, iPhone, or iPod because you can take all of your books everywhere you go. Usually you will get the book cheaper, and it is more portable. If you do not know what to read, go online and search a topic you think will help you grow. For example, if you want to become a world champion fisherman, then search for "books about becoming a great fisherman." You have to be specific about the types of books you read. If you read a fiction book for entertainment, that will not help you grow. It is not wrong to read fiction, but that type of book will not help you succeed.

One of the best quotes that my dad has given me is, "What you become five years from now will be determined by the books that you read and by the people you associate with."

As a reward, my dad gives me $20 for every book that I read. The principle behind his philosophy is that one day I will more than likely be paid according to what I have learned from my reading. I read a statement in a book that the average millionaire reads one book a week while the average American reads less than one book a year. As a kid, make up your mind to refuse to be an average American, but strive to see how many books you can read in a year.

"Readers are leaders." - Anonymous

---

2. People

My parents taught me that you can learn something from everybody, especially people older than you. There is always someone who has gone through something similar to what you have. There will always be someone who has accomplished something similar to your goal. I have found many people that I call mentors which I talked about earlier in this book. Remember, a mentor is someone who can help you get closer to your goal that you respect and will listen to. Some of your mentors may be totally different than others, and that's awesome. You may have different mentors for different areas of your life. I have different mentors for different areas of life, and all of them have helped me become who I am today. To receive the most from your mentors, you always have to be willing to listen and act upon what they are teaching you to do.

Who should be your mentor

I can't necessarily tell you what person to choose as your mentor, but I can give you some ideas of what to look for when deciding on one. He or she should have these 3 qualities:

- Know something about helping you with your dream.

- Have more experience than you in your field.

- Be willing to give of their time.

Important: Your mentor is not someone who would hold you back.

How to get a mentor

Getting a mentor is easy. You just have to find someone who has experience doing something similar to your goal and get in touch with them. You can ask for advice and anytime you need help, call, text, or meet with them. No matter what, you must find one or more people to help you along your path to success.

I remind myself every morning: "Nothing I say this day will teach me anything. So if I'm going to learn, I must do it by listening." - Larry King

3. YouTube

YouTube honestly is one of the most impactful tools available to humans. They could charge $100 a month, and it would be worth it. Why is it so important? YouTube has numerous videos on every topic imaginable, including many videos on how to reach goals. If you want to learn how to become a golfer, there are videos to help you. People who are masters in certain areas constantly put up videos demonstrating how they became successful. They often want to meet important people, but what they may not realize is that we can meet any celebrity through YouTube. YouTube can help you reach your goal just as it has helped me become a much a better baseball player. YouTube can help anyone succeed; people simply take it for granted. Please do not make this mistake. Utilize YouTube. Constantly learn! Constantly grow!

How to go on YouTube

Go to the website, youtube.com or download a YouTube app.

4. Articles on the Internet

If you get your parents' permission, I recommend finding articles on the Internet that will help you with your goal. Articles have helped me learn a lot, and I think they will work for you also. The benefit is that they are short but have a lot of tips that will help you.

Where to find articles

Simply open the Google search tab and type in "articles about (any topic)," and articles will come up.

5. CD's and Podcasts

CD's and podcasts have the same benefits, so I included them together. They are important because the more you can listen to success stories, the more success will be in your mind. My dad and I constantly have something playing that will motivate us to be successful. The more you hear, the more you learn. So what better way to do that than through listening to CD's and podcasts?

How to get CD's or podcasts

A great source for podcasts is on iTunes. By going to iTunes, you can download podcasts that you can listen to for free. All you have to do is type in the name of the podcast that you want to listen to on iTunes, and whatever is available will come up. As for CD's, they are available online or at a store. I recommend going online and ordering them. As you can see, the Internet is a huge source to help you find the resources you need.

6. God

This is the most important one. God can benefit your life in so many ways. The reason I have peace and true happiness in my life is because I put God first, read the Bible and pray every day, go to church, and serve the poor. God will always be there any time you need help or advice. You can always go to the Bible to look for answers.

How to get God

All you have to do is pray or read the Bible, let God speak to your heart, and your relationship with Him will grow. If you want to know more about Him, simply look for a good church and start attending. You can message me on social media, and I will you find a church in your area.

If you do not have your own resources that you use, I have given you these ideas for starters. Play around with them and find out what helps you grow. Make a list of all the helpful resources that you are committed to do daily and then move on to the next step.

Step 3: Schedule time in the day to use your resources.

This basically just means to make a schedule. Decide how much time you will spend each day on each resource. Say you want to read 15 minutes a day. When you go to bed, ask your parents if they have anything planned for you the next day and if you will be able to have some free time. If they say you will have free time from 4:00-6:00, make sure to find 15 minutes to read during those two hours.

I would suggest that you create your personal growth list. I want you to always find time to do the things on the list. My dad and I make a to-do list each day. The list can change depending on what needs to be done. Some things are on the to-do list every day. Some examples are: watch YouTube (which is a personal growth resource), read (which is a personal growth resource), pray, and connect with God (which is a personal growth resource), etc. The point is, I use my personal growth resources every day, and I schedule time to do them. It is very important to use and do every one of the resources on your list so you can grow.

Step 4: Take notes on what you are learning.

It is very important to take notes on what you are learning because it always helps you remember the things you have been taught. If you learn something in a book or see something you think can help you, write it down and highlight it. Always take notes if you hear someone say something helpful or you watch something good. Write it down and every night, review what you have learned. It will help you remember and will help you grow.

Step 5: Put what you learn into action.

While it is great to learn, you must take what you have been taught and apply it. It has been said, "One action is worth more than a thousand good intentions." In other words, don't just think about your goals; take action to make them happen.

Note: Always desire to learn more and be the person who asks questions. If you want to succeed, being eager to learn is the way to go. You are never good enough or know enough to stop learning.

Chapter 6

Be a Kid With A Mission

In the final chapter of *Keys To Success For Kids,* I would like to share something that God has inspired me to do. God has inspired me to start a program called *Kids With A Mission.* I started this program to simply help kids to grasp the fact that they can make a difference around the world. One of our main goals is to help everyone realize that they are never too young to do anything they put their mind to do. I hope that by the time you reach the end of this book, you will realize that the time is now. Whatever age you are now, you need to start learning, serving, and working at whatever you want to achieve. *Kids With A Mission* has four goals that we want every kid to work on. I'm going to discuss each of the five goals and tell why they are important.

1. Stop bullying

I want everybody reading this book to think about if they have bullied someone, been bullied, or seen someone being bullied. Almost every single person reading this book will most likely answer yes to one of those questions. To me, that shows that bullying in the world is getting worse and worse. There is a verse in the Bible that says, *"Death and life are in the power of the tongue,"* (Proverbs 18:21). You constantly hear stories about people shooting themselves because they are tired of hearing insults and being bullied. These stories show us that there is a major issue of using the tongue as a weapon of death. Because one person said something mean to someone, the other person felt so bad that they literally ended their own life. You may not realize it, but one mean thing you say might end up making someone hate their life to the point of death. Around the world, *Kids With A Mission* is trying to get kids to understand that what they say is very important. After reading this, I want you to set a goal that you will never be mean to someone again. Your words are powerful. But the good news is the Bible didn't just say that there is death in the power of the tongue; it also said there was life, so I challenge you to use your tongue to speak life to others. Just like one word can end up killing someone, one word can also end up changing someone for the good. At *Kids With A Mission*, we realize that we can't completely stop bullying because there will always be someone being mean. But we do believe that we can help change people's lives by simply speaking one word of encouragement.

I challenge you to say one kind thing to three people every day. There are some rules though; every day it has to be a new person. That means if one day you say something nice to your dad, the next day it won't count if you say something nice to your dad again. You can say something nice to him, but you still have to say something nice to three new people. Now say that 100 people read this book and each of them tell three people something nice. That means that 300 people were told something nice about themselves. Now say those 300 people felt so loved by what you said to them that they told three people something nice. That would add another 900 people for a total of 1,200 people who feel loved in one day. When those 1,200 people said something to someone else, then those people said something, and those people said something, then all of a sudden we have impacted the world. So when you tell someone something nice, tell them to tell three people something nice and make sure that those three people tell someone something nice. That way the love has reached across the world. That is the only way that we can come close to stopping bullying.

I am not sure if you have heard of the ALS ice bucket challenge, but basically there is a video someone posts of someone dumping a bucket of water on them, and then they nominate three people to do the same. Then those three people nominate three more people. It keeps going and going. Now I thought it would be cool if we can do a love challenge. I want you to post a video of yourself saying one thing nice about three people. Then those three people have to say something nice about three more people; then those people have to say something nice about three more people, and the challenge keeps going and going until there is no one left to do the challenge. So, go ahead and do the love challenge! Use the hashtag "#LoveChallenge."

2. Help kids who have no father.

It has been said 80% of criminals come from fatherless homes. I really don't have to say any more than that. James 1:7 says that pure religion is to look after the fatherless. God commands us to help the fatherless. One of my personal passions is to buy a new bike or a nice pair of shoes for fatherless kids. Even if you can't buy them stuff, you can always be a friend to the fatherless and be kind to them. Here are four ways that you can help the fatherless:

- Buy them a new bike.

- Invite them to do something fun with you and your family.

- Buy them a nice new pair of shoes.

- Be a friend to them and include them so they feel like they belong.

3. Serve the homeless.

There are 3.5 million homeless in the U.S. alone. God says that what you do to the least of these (meaning the less fortunate), you do unto Me (meaning Jesus). This means, however you treat a homeless person is how you treat God. If you treat a homeless person good, you are treating Jesus good, and if you treat a homeless person badly, you are treating Jesus badly. It is very important to show kindness to them and to make them feel like you care. From the time that I was very young, I have gone with my dad to pass out sleeping bags to the homeless late at night and to give Starbucks coffee to the homeless under the bridge at 5 am. While I may have been nervous at first, I have really grown to enjoy and look forward to giving back to the homeless.

4. End Childhood Obesity

I really hope you pay attention to what I'm about to share. Many kids' health is in extreme danger. Childhood obesity is growing rapidly. I believe that foods affect moods, and moods affect success. So if you want to succeed, you must be healthy. I would like to share some facts before I discuss how to be healthy.

Facts:

1. Only 2% of kids in the U.S. eat healthy daily.

Based on diet recommendations established by the United States Department of Agriculture, only 2% of children have a healthy diet. In fact, in a survey of high school students, only three out of every ten report eating vegetables nearly every day. Of the vegetables consumed, one fourth is in the form of French fries or potato chips.

FYI: We should not consider potato chips as vegetables.

2. Unhealthy kids have a reduced lifespan.

Unless crazy changes occur, experts say that unhealthy children have a reduced life span of 5 years or more.

3. Less exercise, more TV?

Every kid should get at least thirty minutes of exercise daily. The problem is that 25% of kids in the U.S. don't do any exercise at all, but the average kid watches 4-5 hours of TV a day. This is not good for our bodies or our mind.

4. According to statistics, 31.7% of children are overweight.

The Solution:

The good news is that the solution is simpler than you may think. Thankfully the kids reading this book are hearing this early in life. We have seen many people (kids included) who just don't know how to be healthy. That is why I'm writing this to you, so that you can live a healthier and more successful life. By that I mean, a life in which you feel healthy and energetic. Following are some simple steps that will help you become healthier and feel better about yourself.

Drink more water.

One of the main reasons why kids are unhealthy nowadays is because of the amount of soda they drink. Most kids only drink soda and sugary drinks. If you want to be healthy, you should substitute soda with water. When I go to restaurants, I never order soda. Instead, I ask for water with lemon. Water with lemon is a very healthy drink, and I believe it is the healthiest drink you could have. Here are some facts about water with lemon.

- Water with lemon cleanses your system.

- It reduces the risk of being sick.

- It clears your skin.

- It gives you a better mood and helps your success.

- It freshens your breath.

So I encourage you, and I challenge you to drink two glasses of water with lemon per day. You will feel a lot better by drinking water instead of soda.

Warning: Be careful of drinking too many fruit drinks because they are loaded with tons of sugar.

Exercise more, watch less TV.

Many people know exercise is good, but they don't do it or realize the benefits of it. Five benefits of exercise are listed below.

- Helps you lose weight.

- Improves your mood.

- Boosts your energy.

- Helps you sleep better.

- Improves your focus!!!

Not only is exercise good for you, it can also be very fun. I am going to give you some fun ideas for kids to do that can count as exercise and make them healthy.

- Jog or go for a walk

- Sports

- Jump rope or dance aerobics

- Swim

- Go for a bike ride

The great news is that there are so many different ways to exercise. You can choose exercises that you love to do and have fun doing. I challenge you to do thirty minutes of exercise every day and only watch one hour of TV. You will have more energy and will enjoy exercising.

Juice more, eat fast food less.

One day while daydreaming, my thoughts were interrupted when I heard the sound of glass gently hitting the table. I looked up and saw a plate with five different fruits and vegetables on it. I heard my dad say, "Son, from now on I want you to eat five fruits and vegetables a day. We are going to call it your daily five. There are two ways you can eat them. Either you can pick them up and eat them like food or you can juice them." He grabbed the plate and said, "Follow me." He walked over to the kitchen, and I followed him. He pointed to a small machine that had the words *NutriBullet* written on it. Dad said, "This machine is going to help you feel so much better and enjoy a healthy lifestyle." Then I saw him pick up the five fruits and vegetables and toss them in the cup that came with the *NutriBullet,* and he added some water. Then he placed the cup on the machine, and within thirty seconds the fruits and vegetables were completely liquefied. He took the cup off the machine, unscrewed the lid and put a straw in the cup and told me to drink it. After I was done drinking it, he asked me, "What tastes better and was faster? You eating the fruits and vegetables or juicing them?"

I answered, "Juicing them, and it was actually pretty good!"

He replied, "I want you to juice every day. It is very important for you to develop these habits while you are young. It will improve your life when you are older."

From that day on, I have always loved juicing. It has been a big help, and I believe it will help you. If you do not have a juicer, I encourage you to do everything you can to get one and to juice daily. Ask your parents to get a juicer for you and offer to do chores for it. You will not regret it.

If your parents want to know more about juicing, first tell them to go to Amazon.com and pick up a book called "Just Juice It." It was written by my dad, Matt Maddix, and has been a big help to a lot of people. Whatever you do, you need to have a juicer and start as soon as possible. It has literally killed cancer for people and will help you become healthier. I want to answer two questions you might have.

Q. What juicer should I get?

A. NutriBullet

Q. What are some good recipes for juicing?

A. There are endless recipes to try. I encourage you to try as many different ones as you can. As for my favorite recipes, I love pineapple, banana, strawberry, and spinach, but honestly there are so many other juices I like. It is all a matter of opinion.

I encourage you to juice twice a day, and I guarantee you will see a huge difference in your life.

I am going to give you five recommendations that will help you to become healthier. I am challenging you to take these five actions very seriously. You have to commit to these if you want to be successful in life and maintain good health.

- Drink 2-4 glasses of water with lemon a day.

- Exercise thirty minutes a day.

- Juice twice a day.

- Only eat fast food once a week.

- Stay away from sugar and junk food.

This may be a hard jump at first, but in the end it is the best for your health and success. Please challenge your friends to follow this challenge so we can all be healthier and successful.

JOIN THE "KIDS 4 HEALTH" MOVEMENT:

Recently, I started a company called, "Kids 4 Health!" We are on a mission to end Childhood Obesity. As I write this book there are currently over 12.7 MILLION OBESE Children in America and we are on a mission to help empower these kids to realize that they can lose weight and live a healthy lifestyle. Most people have no idea just how bad the negative side effects of obesity in a child's life really are.

Potential Negative Psychological Outcomes:

- *Depression*
- *Low self esteem*
- *Risk for eating disorders*
- *Behavior and Learning problems*
- *Poor body image*

Potential Health Consequences:

- *Type 2 Diabetes*
- *Asthma*
- *Hypertension*
- *Sleep apnea*

- *Cancer*
- *Heart disease*

For these reasons alone, I wake up every morning and work my face off to help every child on planet earth to lose weight and develop healthy habits so that they can enjoy the benefits of living a healthy lifestyle. I guarantee that any kid who joins "Kids 4 Health" will see a major transformation in their life.

The Benefits of "Kids 4 Health" are:

- *Lose Weight*
- *Increase Confidence & Self-Esteem*
- *Less Likely to Get Sick*
- *Perform Better in School*
- *Perform Better in Sports*
- *Feel Better About your Body*
- *Increased Happiness*
- *Sleep Better*
- *Increased Focus*
- *More Positive Attitude & Energy*

Go to kids4health.tv and watch my video of how you can join the movement. If you know any kid that is depressed, over weight or currently in need of empowerment, please get my book in their hands with urgency.

You can help *Kids With A Mission* by simply going to the *Kids With A Mission* Facebook page, and simply like and share what you were doing to change the world. *Kids With A Mission* is a place where kids can go to realize we all are working together to make the world a much better place. You can also email us at calebmaddix@gmail.com and send pictures of what you have been doing so we can better motivate kids to change the world.

Every key I've given you in this book will help you succeed and not only reach your goals, but also go far past what you ever thought was possible. I hope this book has changed the way you look at life and the way you go about it. I don't want this to be the last time we connect. I have created my own Facebook page for kids to go to get weekly motivation and tips to keep straight on the path of success.

Below are ways to connect, and I hope this book has impacted you and we can stay in touch. Thank you for reading it. Don't forget to follow each of these tips and please, if this book has impacted you, tell others about it and let us know how you are doing and how your life has improved. The last thing I have to say is to ALWAYS be a KID...WITH...A...MISSION!

To have Caleb Maddix for a speaking engagement or kid's coaching session, contact the author, Caleb Maddix, at the following:

Website: calebmaddix.tv

Facebook: Caleb Maddix

Twitter: @CalebMaddix

Instagram: Calebmaddix and also KidsWithAMission

Email: Calebmaddix@gmail.com

About the Author

Caleb Maddix lives in St. Petersburg, FL. He is thirteen years old and in the eighth grade. Caleb is a homeschooler. He is also an author, public speaker, life coach, baseball player, entrepreneur, and founder of *Kids with a Mission*. Caleb has a dream to help millions of fatherless kids, the homeless, and children suffering with obesity. He is very focused on personal growth and reads an average of one book per week. Caleb is Co-Host of "Maddix Motivations," and Founder of "Kids 4 Health!" Caleb is passionate about God, his family, hanging out with his friends, serving the homeless, and playing baseball. Caleb has a strong work ethic and is laser focused on impacting millions of kids and teenagers across the world.

Made in the USA
Lexington, KY
26 December 2015